GOD'S PROMISE OF
HAPPINESS

GOD'S PROMISE OF
HAPPINESS

RANDY
ALCORN

Tyndale House Publishers, Inc., Carol Stream, Illinois

Visit Tyndale online at www.tyndale.com.

TYNDALE and Tyndale's quill logo are registered trademarks of Tyndale House Publishers, Inc.

God's Promise of Happiness

Designed by Jennifer Ghionzoli

Edited by Stephanie Rische

ISBN 978-1-4964-1145-7

Printed in the United States of America

21	20	19	18	17	16	15
7	6	5	4	3	2	1

CONTENTS

THE HAPPINESS GOD OFFERS

My dear brothers and sisters, if anybody in the world ought to be happy, we are the people. . . . How boundless our privileges! How brilliant our hopes!

CHARLES SPURGEON

Do we seek happiness because we're sinners or because we're human? Should faith in God be dragged forward by duty or propelled by delight? Must we choose between holiness and happiness?

Much of my time with my wife, Nanci, and our family and friends is filled with fun and laughter. The God we love is the enemy of sin *and* the creator of pleasure and humor. (True, God's gifts of art, movies, books, sports, work, food, drink, sex, and money can all be used selfishly and sinfully. In a fallen world, what *can't* be?)

I was an empty, unhappy teenager when I first heard the Good News about Jesus. Soon I put my trust in him and experienced a deep, heart-felt happiness unlike anything I'd ever known. Nevertheless, there's a paradigm-shifting doctrine I was never taught in church, Bible college, or seminary: the happiness of God. Scripture says about Christ, "Whoever says he abides in him ought to walk in the same way in which he walked" (1 John 2:6). If Jesus walked around mostly miserable, it makes sense that we would. But if he was happy, shouldn't we be happy too?

Christians throughout church history understood that happiness, gladness, feasting, and partying are God's gifts, yet many Christians today live as if faith drains happiness! Life isn't easy, of course, but believers have the benefit of walking the hard roads hand in hand with a Savior and King whose love for us is immeasurable. Who has more reason to be happy than we do?

There are a lot of promises in this booklet—most of them are God's, not mine. All his promises are fully trustworthy. Why? Because they're blood-bought, paid for by an all-powerful Lord who loves you radically.

Ask your Creator to speak to you, especially as

you contemplate the Scripture I've included. May you find greater happiness in God than you've ever known—beginning now and never ending.

> *The people ransomed by the LORD . . . will come to Zion singing with joy. Everlasting happiness will be on their heads as a crown. They will be glad and joyful. They will have no sorrow or grief.*
>
> ISAIAH 35:10, GW

Randy Alcorn
FALL 2015

CHAPTER 1

OUR UNIVERSAL SEARCH FOR HAPPINESS

⁓

DO WE HAVE A CHOICE WHETHER OR NOT TO DESIRE HAPPINESS?

Augustine wrote in the fifth century, "Every man, whatsoever his condition, desires to be happy."[1]

Nearly 1,300 years later, the French philosopher and mathematician Blaise Pascal wrote, "All men seek happiness. This is without exception. . . . The will never takes the least step but to this object. This is the motive of every action of every man, even of those who hang themselves."[2]

Puritan Thomas Manton said, "It is as natural for the reasonable creature to desire to be happy, as it is for the fire to burn."[3] J. C. Ryle said, "All men naturally hunger and thirst after happiness."[4]

If we don't understand what these wise people

knew, we'll imagine people have a choice whether or not to pursue happiness. *We don't.* Happiness-seeking is built into every person, of every age and circumstance.

I believe we inherited from our Eden-dwelling ancestors a sense of their pre-Fall happiness. Our hearts refuse to settle for sin, suffering, boredom, and purposelessness—we long for something better. Were we merely the product of natural selection and survival of the fittest, we'd have no grounds for believing any ancient happiness existed. But we are all nostalgic for an Eden we've only seen fleeting hints of.

Unfortunately, for countless Christians, being happy yields an uneasy guilt. Being holy is something we can do in God's presence, but being happy is something we're more comfortable doing behind his back (which isn't possible). But God's children are told to be happy "before the LORD":

- You shall rejoice before the LORD your God, you and your sons and your daughters. (Deuteronomy 12:12)

- May all those who seek you be happy and rejoice in you! (Psalm 40:16, NET)

IS IT OKAY FOR CHRISTIANS TO BE HAPPY?

Shout triumphantly to the LORD, all the earth! Be happy! Rejoice out loud!

PSALM 98:4, CEB

It's not just okay to be happy; it's *right* to be happy. The Bible clearly *tells* God's children to be happy. Jesus commanded his disciples to be happy, and for a compelling reason: "Rejoice that your names are written in heaven" (Luke 10:20). If we're not experiencing happiness in God, then we're disobeying and missing the abundant life Jesus came to give (see John 10:10).

We shouldn't criticize people for wanting to be happy. Pastors who encourage people to stop seeking happiness or parents who don't want their children motivated by happiness are fighting a losing battle. They'll never succeed, and they'll do damage by distancing the gospel from the happiness everyone craves.

Consistently seeking our happiness in Jesus shouts to everyone that God is present and working in the world and that he'll one day reign over a new universe. As A. W. Tozer said, "The people of God ought to be the happiest people in all the wide world!"[5]

- Be happy and shout to God who makes us strong! (Psalm 81:1, CEV)
- Always be full of joy in the Lord. I say it again—rejoice! (Philippians 4:4, NLT)

DOES THE BIBLE HAVE MUCH TO SAY ABOUT HAPPINESS?

There are more than 2,700 passages in the Bible containing words such as *joy, happiness, gladness, merriment, pleasure, cheer, laughter, delight, jubilation, feasting, exultation,* and *celebration.*

God makes it clear that seeking happiness through sin is wrong and fruitless. But seeking happiness in him is good and right:

- Happy are you, O Israel! Who is like you, a people saved by the LORD! (Deuteronomy 33:29)

- Be happy and excited! You will have a great
  reward in heaven. (Matthew 5:12, CEV)

Many passages don't contain the word *happiness*, but the concept is unmistakable:

- May Yahweh bless you and protect you;
  may Yahweh make His face shine on you
  and be gracious to you; may Yahweh look
  with favor on you and give you peace.
  (Numbers 6:24-26, HCSB)
- All the days of the afflicted are evil, but
  the cheerful of heart has a continual feast.
  (Proverbs 15:15)
- Enjoy life with the wife whom you love.
  (Ecclesiastes 9:9)

DOESN'T THE BIBLE TALK ABOUT JOY RATHER THAN HAPPINESS?

An ungrounded separation of joy from happiness
has infiltrated the Christian community. Among
English speakers, the word *happiness* has been a
bridge between the church and the world, until
recently. It's a bridge we can't afford to burn. *Joy* is

a perfectly good word. But there are other equally good words that Bible translators use to convey happiness, including *gladness, merriment, delight,* and *pleasure.*

Happiness and joy are synonyms. They're much more alike than unalike. *Joy,* in Merriam-Webster's dictionary, is defined as "a feeling of great happiness" and "a source or cause of great happiness."[6]

Similarly, look in Hebrew and Greek lexicons at the many different words translated *joyful, glad, merry,* and *delighted.* In nearly every case, you'll find these words defined as meaning "happy."

Think of expressions using the word joy:

- "He jumped for joy."
- "She's our pride and joy."
- "I wept for joy."

In each case, isn't joy synonymous with happiness?

John Piper writes, "If you have nice little categories for 'joy is what Christians have' and 'happiness is what the world has,' you can scrap those when you go to the Bible, because the Bible is indiscriminate in its uses of the language of happiness and joy and contentment and satisfaction."[7]

- You, O LORD, have made me *happy* by your work. I will sing for *joy* because of what you have done. (Psalm 92:4, NET)
- God, you have caused the nation to grow and made the people *happy*. And they have shown their *happiness* to you, like the *joy* during harvest time. (Isaiah 9:3, NCV)

ARE THERE BIG DIFFERENCES BETWEEN *JOY* AND *HAPPINESS*?

Until the twentieth century, *happiness* and *joy* were used interchangeably. Then some Christian leaders saw the word *happiness* used for sinful activities (e.g., people abandoning their families to "be happy"), so they started speaking against happiness-seeking.

Their concern was understandable, yet what they should have said was, "God built us to desire happiness, but we're to seek happiness in him!"

Depicting joy in contrast with happiness has obscured the true meaning of both words. Aren't joyful people typically cheerful—smiling and laughing a lot? They're *happy*!

I agree with Joni Eareckson Tada:

> We're often taught to be careful of the difference between joy and happiness. Happiness, it is said, is an emotion that depends upon what "happens." Joy by contrast, is supposed to be enduring, stemming deep from within our soul and which is not affected by the circumstances surrounding us. . . . I don't think God had any such hair-splitting in mind. Scripture uses the terms interchangeably along with words like delight, gladness, blessed. There is no scale of relative spiritual values applied to any of these.[8]

Here's a sampling of the more than one hundred Bible verses in various translations that use *joy* and *happiness* together with obviously parallel meanings:

- For the Jews it was a time of *happiness* and *joy*, gladness and honor. (Esther 8:16, NIV)

- Give your father and mother *joy*! May she who gave you birth be *happy*. (Proverbs 23:25, NLT)
- The young women will rejoice with dancing, while young and old men rejoice together. I will turn their mourning into *joy* . . . and bring *happiness* out of grief. (Jeremiah 31:13, HCSB)

WITH SO MANY DIFFERENT TRANSLATIONS, HOW CAN WE BE SURE OF WHAT THE BIBLE REALLY SAYS ABOUT HAPPINESS?

The Bible was written almost entirely in Hebrew and Greek. Later, it was carefully translated into languages, including English, by teams of rigorously trained scholars. While they often use different words, the many English translations aren't nearly as different in meaning as is often supposed.

Consider Ecclesiastes 9:7. The New American Standard Bible reads, "Eat your bread in happiness and drink your wine with a *cheerful* heart." Other than using *your* instead of *thy*, the English Standard

Version reads the same as the King James Version: "Eat your bread with joy, and drink your wine with a *merry* heart." The New International Version says, "Eat your food with *gladness*, and drink your wine with a *joyful* heart."

Don't think these translations disagree on the meanings of the original Hebrew. They align very closely. Why? Because the two Hebrew words are synonyms, and each can be accurately rendered by any of the chosen English words—also synonyms.

The New Living Translation, the Complete Jewish Bible, and the New English Translation all agree on another rendering of the last part of Ecclesiastes 9:7: "Drink your wine with a *happy* heart" (emphasis added). *Happy* is a different word from *cheerful*, *merry*, or *joyful*, but it has the same essential meaning—hence, none of these translations contradicts the others.

Is only one translation right? No, because *exact* equivalents rarely exist between languages—and Hebrew into English is no exception. As long as the translations effectively capture the original's intent, all are correct, despite the different wording.

WHAT DOES *BLESSED* HAVE TO DO WITH BEING HAPPY?

Growing up in an unbelieving home, I never heard the word *blessed*. After coming to Christ and beginning to attend church, I heard it countless times. I didn't know its meaning; it just sounded holy and spiritual.

Years later, studying Greek in college, I heard someone say that *blessed* in the English Bible often really means "happy." My response was, "Huh?" Everyone knows it's good to be blessed, but it certainly didn't sound like happy to me!

The Hebrew word *asher* is used twenty-six times in the Psalms alone. When the Jewish people heard Psalm 1 read, they heard "*Happy* is the one who . . ."

Jesus used the Greek word *makarios* nine times in the Beatitudes, which meant to the original listeners, "*Happy* are the poor in spirit. . . . *Happy* are the meek. . . . *Happy* are the merciful. . . . *Happy* are the peacemakers," and so on (Matthew 5:3-12).

Young's Literal Translation, the Common English Bible, the Jerusalem Bible, the Phillips New Testament, and the Good News Translation all translate *makarios* as "happy" the great majority of the time. My extensive research and dialogue with Hebrew and Greek scholars and translators left me perplexed over why many translators continue to use the word *blessed* as a translation of *asher* and *makarios*. Four hundred years ago, when the King James Version was translated, *blessed* still meant "happy." But to most people today, it means something quite different.

The fact is, some modern versions remain reluctant to change the translation of particularly familiar verses in the King James Version, and few are more familiar than the Beatitudes. Had the Bible never before been translated into English, would modern scholars even consider rendering *asher* or *makarios* as "blessed"? It's hard to imagine they would.

- How happy [*asher*] is the man who does not follow the advice of the wicked or take the path of sinners or join a group of mockers! Instead, his delight is in the LORD's instruction, and he meditates on it day and night. (Psalm 1:1-2, HCSB)

- Happy [*makarios*] are people who are hopeless, because the kingdom of heaven is theirs. Happy [*makarios*] are people who grieve, because they will be made glad. Happy [*makarios*] are people who are humble, because they will inherit the earth. (Matthew 5:3-5, CEB)

WHAT MAKES PEOPLE GENUINELY HAPPY?

Both psychological research and Scripture demonstrate that those who give generously and serve others are happy people. Those waiting to be happy shouldn't hold their breath—it could be a long wait!

A 2010 survey of 4,500 American adults revealed that of those who volunteered an average of one hundred hours a year, 68 percent reported they were physically healthier, 73 percent said it "lowered my stress levels," and 89 percent said it "has improved my sense of well-being."[9]

God's gift of happiness for believers is more than simply recognizing that happiness comes from knowing, loving, and serving God. We must *do something*: open God's Word; go to a Bible study; join a church; volunteer at a homeless shelter; write a check to support missions.

Our happiness was bought and paid for by Jesus. But it's ours only when we take hold of the gift God paid a tremendous price for!

- Happy is a man who finds wisdom and who acquires understanding. (Proverbs 3:13, HCSB)
- Day after day they met together in the temple. They broke bread together in different homes and shared their food happily and freely. (Acts 2:46, CEV)

HOW MANY PEOPLE ARE REALLY HAPPY?

Although the quest for happiness isn't new, people today seem particularly thirsty for it. Our culture is characterized by increased depression and anxiety, particularly among the young.[10] Numerous Christians live in daily sadness, anger, anxiety, or loneliness, taken captive by their circumstances. They lose joy over traffic jams, long lines, or increased gas prices, missing the reasons for happiness expressed on nearly every page of Scripture.

Research indicates there is "little correlation between the circumstances of people's lives and how happy they are."[11] Yet when people respond to the question "Why aren't you happy?" they tend to focus on their current circumstances. Happy people look to Someone so big that by his grace, even great difficulties provide opportunities for a deeper kind of happiness.

> *Trust in the LORD, and do good; dwell in the land and befriend faithfulness. Delight yourself in the LORD, and he will give you the desires of your heart.*
>
> PSALM 37:3-4

IS THERE ANY DIFFERENCE BETWEEN A BELIEVER'S AND AN UNBELIEVER'S HAPPINESS?

No and yes. The apostle Paul said to unbelievers that God "did good by giving you rains from heaven and fruitful seasons, satisfying your hearts with food and gladness" (Acts 14:17). So God extends his common grace to all people, bringing a certain amount of happiness to everyone—enough to give a taste of what is so often missing.

When an atheist enjoys the cool breeze of a sunny autumn day as he writes his treatise saying God doesn't exist, the ultimate source of his pleasure remains God. God is the author of the universe itself—including the powers of rational thought the atheist misuses to argue against God.

David Murray identifies six kinds of happiness available to unbelievers and believers alike: social, natural, vocational, physical, intellectual, and humorous. The one remaining component, available only to believers, is spiritual happiness. Murray calls that unique happiness "a joy that at times contains more pleasure and delight than the other six put together."[12]

A key to enjoying the Christian life is connecting the dots between our happiness and God's provision. When I run with my dog or look at Jupiter dominating the sky over Mount Hood, I experience happiness. Unbelievers are capable of enjoying happiness in the same things, but their happiness can't be as immense or enduring because they're disconnected from the Provider.

- You will show me the path of life; in Your presence is fullness of joy; at Your right hand are pleasures forevermore. (Psalm 16:11, NKJV)
- How priceless is your unfailing love, O God! People take refuge in the shadow of your wings. They feast on the abundance of your house; you give them drink from your river of delights. (Psalm 36:7-8, NIV)

WHY DOES HAPPINESS SEEM ELUSIVE?

For many people, happiness changes with the winds of circumstance. We can't count on such happiness tomorrow, much less forever.

We say to ourselves, *I'll be happy when* . . . Yet either we don't get what we want and are unhappy, or we do get what we want and are still unhappy.

Sometimes happiness eludes us because we demand perfection in an imperfect world. Everything must be "just right," or we're unhappy. And nothing is ever just right! So we don't enjoy the ordinary days that are a little or even mostly right.

The Bible is clear—this life is temporary, but

we *will* live forever somewhere, in a far better or far worse place. (For those who know Christ, this life is the closest we'll ever come to Hell; for those who don't know Christ, it's the closest they'll ever come to Heaven.)

Looking at life through the lens of Christ's redemptive work for us, reasons for happiness abound.

> *Know therefore that the LORD your God is God, the faithful God who keeps covenant and steadfast love with those who love him and keep his commandments, to a thousand generations.*
>
> DEUTERONOMY 7:9

SHOULD WE EXPECT HAPPINESS TO COME EASILY AND TO ALWAYS LAST?

It's unrealistic to expect perpetual happiness while the Curse is in effect. But the day is coming when "there will no longer be any curse" (Revelation 22:3, HCSB). Believing this can front-load our eternal happiness to the lives we live today.

I'm not always happy, any more than I'm always

holy. But by God's grace, I'm happier in Christ now than I've ever been. And I've learned to make choices that increase my joy. Great pain certainly dulls—and at times overshadows—happiness, but it can't destroy what's grounded in our ever-faithful God.

Nanci and I give each other permission to experience sadness when we hear bad news. We don't pretend all is well. But knowing God's commands to rejoice in him through his all-sufficient power, we meditate on his Word and call on him to impart his gladness to us. In time God exchanges our natural responses with his supernatural, joy-giving presence. Sometimes sorrow and joy do battle; sometimes they coexist, but when our hearts and minds are on Christ, joy is never far away:

- You [LORD] changed my sorrow into dancing. You took away my clothes of sadness, and clothed me in happiness. (Psalm 30:11, NCV)
- [Jesus said,] "I have said these things to you, that in me you may have peace. In

the world you will have tribulation. But take heart; I have overcome the world." (John 16:33)

IS GOD SERIOUS ABOUT OFFERING US HAPPINESS?

Jesus tells two stories about great parties thrown by God: the wedding feast (see Matthew 22:1-14) and the great banquet (see Luke 14:15-24). In both celebrations, the host (representing God) invites guests to join in.

People in that culture knew how to throw parties, and nothing was more festive than a wedding feast—lots of food, drinks, music, and laughter.

In the second story, when a good, happy king with vast wealth threw a party, those the king invited made all kinds of excuses. They refused the invitation. *They said no to happiness.* (If you're too busy for a great wedding feast and the King's banquet, you're too busy!)

These parables exemplify God's sincere invitation to happiness and our tendency to pursue other things we imagine will make us happier.

We couldn't be more wrong. Rejecting the

King's offer of endless celebration in his presence is rejecting happiness itself.

The moral of the story? When God invites you to a party, *say yes.* You'll be happy you did!

> *When the LORD brought us back to Jerusalem, it was like a dream! How we laughed, how we sang for joy! . . . Indeed he did great things for us; how happy we were!*
>
> PSALM 126:1-3, GNT

CAN LASTING HAPPINESS BE FOUND APART FROM GOD?

Oxford professor C. S. Lewis was an atheist and agnostic before believing in Christ. He said,

> God made us: invented us as a man invents an engine. A car is made to run on petrol, and it would not run properly on anything else. Now God designed the human machine to run on Himself. He Himself is the fuel our spirits were designed to burn, or the food our spirits were designed to feed on. There is no

other. That is why it is just no good asking God to make us happy in our own way. . . . God cannot give us a happiness and peace apart from Himself, because it is not there. There is no such thing.[13]

Seeking happiness without God is like seeking water without wetness or sun without light. As fallen, rebellious creatures, while we still want happiness, we don't even *want* to want God. In spiritual darkness, we attribute our happiness to everything but God. But when we know Christ, we can cultivate our awareness of God as the Source of all happiness. Every flower, cup of coffee, meal, and song can stir within us gratitude and happiness.

Because of God's kindness, people can reject God but still receive the benefits of his common grace, including the enjoyment of loving relationships, natural and artistic beauty, and pleasure. However, beware: we live on borrowed time.

In the end, we have two choices:

1. *both* God and happiness
2. *neither* God nor happiness

What we can't have is God without happiness or eternal happiness without God.

- Everyone must die once, and after that be judged by God. In the same manner Christ also was offered in sacrifice once to take away the sins of many. He will appear a second time, not to deal with sin, but to save those who are waiting for him. (Hebrews 9:27-28, GNT)
- Nothing evil will be allowed to enter [Heaven] . . . but only those whose names are written in the Lamb's Book of Life. (Revelation 21:27, NLT)

CHAPTER 2

GOD, JESUS, AND HAPPINESS

DOES THE BIBLE SAY GOD IS HAPPY?

Short answer: Yes.

The apostle Paul wrote of "the gospel of the glory of the blessed [*makarios*] God with which I have been entrusted" (1 Timothy 1:11).

At the end of 1 Timothy, he refers to God as "he who is the blessed [*makarios*] and only Sovereign, the King of kings and Lord of lords" (6:15).

There's that word *blessed* again! Language scholars and lexicons attest that the Greek adjective *makarios*, translated here as "blessed," actually means "happy." For instance,

- "The word translated 'blessed' here [1 Timothy 1:11] . . . means 'happy.' . . .

We have a happy God, a happy Ruler . . . altogether happy and altogether powerful."[14]

- "The term 'blessed' indicates . . . *supreme happiness*."[15]

In 1611, when King James translators chose "blessed," it meant "happy." In fact, the 1828 edition of Noah Webster's dictionary defines *blessed* as "made happy or prosperous; extolled; pronounced happy . . . happy . . . enjoying spiritual happiness and the favor of God; enjoying heavenly felicity."[16]

Likewise, Webster defined *blessedly* as "happily" and *blessedness* as "happiness." Two hundred years ago, people still understood *blessed* to mean "happy."

In contrast, a poll I did of more than one thousand people, mostly Christians, indicated that only 12 percent of them associate *blessed* with *happy*. Most others think of *blessed* not as a happiness word but as a holiness word.

First Timothy 1:11 and 6:15 actually speak of the gospel of the "*happy* God" and the God "who is the *happy* and only Sovereign."

Charles Spurgeon said of 1 Timothy 1:11, "The

Gospel is also the Gospel of happiness. It is called 'the glorious Gospel of the blessed God.' A more correct translation would be, 'the happy God.' Well, then, adorn the Gospel by being happy!"[17]

Every time God calls upon us to be happy, our happiness comes from him:

- *Happy* are the people who know the *joyful* shout; Yahweh, they walk in the light of Your presence. (Psalm 89:15, HCSB)
- Sing, Jerusalem. Israel, shout for *joy*! Jerusalem, be *happy* and *rejoice* with all your heart. (Zephaniah 3:14, NCV)

IS GOD BY NATURE HAPPY OR UNHAPPY?

I'm convinced most people view God as typically unhappy. They think, *Maybe he has occasional moments of happiness, but because we sin we make God unhappy over and over.*

But this logic begins in the wrong place—with us. We flatter ourselves by imagining *we* are the primary source of God's happiness, tilting him one way or the other by what we think, do, and say.

Sure, God can be happy or unhappy with a

person's thoughts or actions, just as a man who's thoroughly happy with his family and life in general can still be unhappy with someone else. However, the Father, Son, and Holy Spirit can never be disappointed with each other. They'll always bring only happiness to one another forever.

If there's ever been a day in history when the happiness of Father, Son, and Holy Spirit was disturbed, surely it would've been on Good Friday. But even then, the triune God knew that the unhappy suffering and death of Jesus ultimately guaranteed for God's children the abolition of death (see 2 Timothy 1:10) and suffering (see Revelation 21:4). It purchased eternal happiness for all who trust in Jesus.

- I know that you [O LORD] . . . are pleased with people of integrity. (1 Chronicles 29:17, GNT)
- This is my beloved Son, with whom I am well pleased. (Matthew 3:17)

DOES IT REALLY MATTER WHETHER GOD IS HAPPY?
It could hardly matter more! An unhappy God would never take pains to provide the everlasting

happiness of his creatures. We'd never ask for or expect grace from an ungracious God, kindness from an unkind God, or happiness from an unhappy God.

If God weren't happy, he couldn't be the Source to give us what we most desire. At best, he might deliver us from Hell's miseries. But Heaven can overflow with happiness only if God himself does.

- The LORD has filled my heart with *joy*; how *happy* I am because of what he has done!" (1 Samuel 2:1, GNT)
- Satisfy us in the morning with your loyal love! Then we will shout for *joy* and be *happy* all our days! (Psalm 90:14, NET)

HOW CAN GOD BE HAPPY WITH HIMSELF AND SEEK HIS OWN GLORY WITHOUT BEING ARROGANT?

The doctrine of the Trinity explains how God can appropriately be God centered and happy with himself. First, because he's praiseworthy. Second, because he properly exalts what's praiseworthy. Third, because each person of the Trinity is others centered, delighting in one another. Jesus said,

"Father . . . you loved me before the creation of the world" (John 17:24, NIV).

Why would a happy God create us if he didn't need us in order to be happy? Jonathan Edwards offered this answer: "It is no defect in a fountain that it is prone to overflow."[18]

When concert attendees give a standing ovation, don't they expect the composer, director, and orchestra members to be happy? The performers find happiness in the audience's happiness.

Surely it's not always selfish to want to make people happy! So why should it disappoint us that God would be happy to receive the praise that makes us happy when we offer it?

John Piper says, "God is the one being in the universe for whom self-exaltation is not the act of a needy ego, but an act of infinite giving. The reason God seeks our praise is not because he won't be fully God until he *gets* it, but that we won't be happy until we *give* it. This is not arrogance. This is grace."[19]

For my name's sake I defer my anger, for the sake of my praise. . . . For my own sake, for

my own sake, I do it. . . . My glory I will
not give to another.

ISAIAH 48:9, 11

WHAT DOES GOD MEAN WHEN HE INVITES US TO SHARE HIS HAPPINESS?

When Jesus said, "Come and share your master's happiness!" (Matthew 25:23, NIV), his message was unmistakable: (1) *God is happy* and (2) *God wants us to join in his happiness.*

Visualize an estate owner who somehow exists as three persons. Suppose his guests are allowed to watch these three enjoying each other's company with eternal, infinite happiness. Now imagine the guests are invited to enter into this delightful relationship.

This is what God has done. Along with countless other children of the King, we'll celebrate God without end and be happy *with* and *in* him.

It would be easy to think the perfect Father, Son, and Spirit wouldn't want to include others in their inner circle of happiness. Who'd believe they would invite us, mere creatures, to share the benefits of their eternally rich relationship? Yet that's exactly what they've done!

Jesus said,

> *I have given [my disciples] the glory you gave me, so they may be one as we are one. . . . May they experience such perfect unity that the world will know that you sent me and that you love them as much as you love me. . . . Then they can see all the glory you gave me because you loved me even before the world began!*
>
> JOHN 17:22-24, NLT

DO WE HAVE TO CHOOSE BETWEEN GOD AND HAPPINESS?

Given this choice, people will choose happiness. But it's a false dichotomy. Happiness can be found only in an eternally happy God.

I like being with happy people—who doesn't? If God weren't happy, living with him forever couldn't possibly appeal to us. God's happiness has significant implications for whether the gospel will be seen as truly good news. If we view

God as an eternally happy God who willingly sacrificed himself to purchase our eternal happiness, we'll realize we can choose both God and happiness, rather than one instead of the other.

I want to spend not only eternity but also my present life accompanied, indwelt, and empowered by a happy God who understands my desire for happiness and can fulfill my dreams of happiness because he is happy.

Fortunately God's happiness isn't just wishful thinking; it's revealed truth!

- You [Lord] make him happy with the joy of your presence. (Psalm 21:6, CEB)
- You don't see [Christ] now, but you believe in him. You are extremely happy with joy and praise. (1 Peter 1:8, GW)

HOW HAPPY IS GOD ABOUT OUR REPENTANCE?

One of the most dramatic pictures of God's happiness is in response to the repentance of his children, in which he lavishes them with grace.

Jesus pictures God as a shepherd who calls together his friends and neighbors, saying, "Rejoice with me, for I have found my sheep that was lost" (Luke 15:6). The Good News Translation reads, "I am so happy I found my lost sheep. Let us celebrate!"

In Christ's parable of the lost son, who is it that runs to his son, embraces him, and forgives him? The father, who represents God. Who orders a feast and fills his home with music and dancing? God.

Believing happiness could be found away from the moral constraints of his family, the young man searched for happiness yet found misery. Desperate, he returns, only to receive from his father the very happiness he was searching for.

The eldest son resents his father for graciously celebrating his brother's repentance. The father explains, "But we had to celebrate and be happy, because your brother was dead, but now he is alive; he was lost, but now he has been found" (Luke 15:32, GNT).

Why did the father say he *had* to celebrate and be happy? Because he's true to his nature—*his happiness compels celebration.* He grieves over sin. But when we repent, he throws a party that all

Heaven joins in. *All because God is happy, enjoys being happy, and wants us to enjoy happiness too!*

- Happy is the person whom the LORD does not consider guilty. (Psalm 32:2, NCV)
- Just so, I tell you, there will be more joy in heaven over one sinner who repents than over ninety-nine righteous persons who need no repentance. (Luke 15:7)

HOW HAPPY IS GOD WITH HIS CREATION?

God is pleased with his creation:

God saw everything that he had made, and behold, it was very good.

GENESIS 1:31

The creation is glad in its Creator:

Let the heavens rejoice, let the earth be glad; let the sea resound, and all that is in it. Let the fields be jubilant, and everything in them; let all the trees of the forest sing for joy.

PSALM 96:11-12, NIV

Listen to God's voice concerning just one of his creations:

> *Do you give the horse his might? Do you*
> *clothe his neck with a mane? . . . He paws*
> *in the valley and exults in his strength. . . .*
> *He laughs at fear and is not dismayed.*
> JOB 39:19, 21-22

Isn't God's utter delight in horses obvious? Since he finds pleasure and happiness in animals, we shouldn't feel "unspiritual" when we do. You may not know God, but if you love animals, you have something in common with their Creator!

A. W. Tozer said, "God is not only . . . happy in His work of creating and redeeming, but He is also enthusiastic. . . . Somebody is having a good time in heaven and earth and sea and sky. Somebody is painting the sky . . . causing . . . the birds to sing. . . . Somebody's running the universe."[20]

God delights even more in the human beings made in his likeness. This statement of God's tender love contains four different Hebrew words for happiness. Note that each describes God's happy feelings:

> *The LORD your God is in your midst, a*
> *mighty one who will save; he will rejoice*
> *over you with gladness; he will quiet you*
> *by his love; he will exult over you with*
> *loud singing.*
>
> ZEPHANIAH 3:17

There's more of the happiness, tenderness, and love of God in this single verse than we can comprehend.

Here's a sampling of verses that talk about God being pleased with his children:

- God "takes pleasure" in those who fear him and hope in his mercy. (Psalm 147:11, NKJV)
- God "will be pleased because of you, just as a husband is pleased with his bride." (Isaiah 62:5, CEV)
- God is pleased when we trust and seek him: "Without faith it is impossible to please him." (Hebrews 11:6)

WAS JESUS HAPPY?

Ask a random group of believers and unbelievers, "Who is the happiest human being who ever lived?" and few would give the correct answer: "Jesus." Consider Psalm 45:6-7, quoted in direct reference to the Messiah in Hebrews 1:8-9, where the Father says of his Son: "Your God . . . made you happier than any of your friends" (CEV).

"Friends" could refer to his immediate group of companions or all fellow human beings. If the latter, he has gladness that exceeds that of all people (which makes sense, because he created us).

Children loved Jesus and were drawn to him—and children are never drawn to killjoys! Matthew describes this scene:

> *Children were brought to him that he*
> *might lay his hands on them and pray.*
> *The disciples rebuked the people, but Jesus*
> *said, "Let the little children come to me*
> *and do not hinder them, for to such belongs*
> *the kingdom of heaven."*
>
> MATTHEW 19:13-14

In the first-ever gospel message of the newborn church, the apostle Peter preached that Psalm 16 is about Christ:

> *David says concerning him, "I saw the*
> *Lord always before me, for he is at my right*
> *hand that I may not be shaken; therefore*
> *my heart was glad, and my tongue rejoiced.*
> *. . . For you will not abandon my soul to*
> *Hades, or let your Holy One see corruption.*
> *. . . You will make me full of gladness with*
> *your presence."*
>
> ACTS 2:25-28, EMPHASIS ADDED

Peter, full of the Holy Spirit, affirmed three times the happiness of Jesus! Yet how many people have ever heard a modern evangelistic message that states, much less emphasizes, that Jesus is happy? Or that what Jesus did on the cross was for the sake of never-ending happiness—ours and his?

> *Jesus, the founder and perfecter of our faith,*
> *who for the joy that was set before him*
> *endured the cross, despising the shame, and is*
> *seated at the right hand of the throne of God.*
>
> HEBREWS 12:2

IF JESUS WAS HAPPY, WHY WAS HE CALLED "A MAN OF SORROWS"?

Regarding Jesus' death, we're told, "He was despised and rejected by men; a man of sorrows, and acquainted with grief" (Isaiah 53:3). He's called "a man of sorrows" not in general but specifically in relationship to his sacrificial work.

As he went to the cross, Jesus said, "My soul is deeply grieved to the point of death" (Mark 14:34, NASB). But he lived more than twelve thousand days, and this was the worst twenty-four hours of his life—experiencing history's most terrible death.

Given the price he paid for our sins, does being "a man of sorrows" in his atoning work contradict the notion Jesus was happy? Absolutely not. Sorrow and happiness can and do coexist within the same person.

Jesus understood that the basis for his sorrow was temporary, while the basis for his gladness was and is permanent. He'd known unbounded happiness before the dawn of time, and he knew it awaited him again.

When Jesus walked the Earth, he lived with

divine happiness in his past, the happiness of an eternal perspective in his present, and the anticipation of unending happiness in the future. Many scholars identify the personification of Wisdom in Proverbs 8 as none other than the person of Christ, who says of the Father,

> *I was his daily source of joy, always happy*
> *in his presence—happy with the world and*
> *pleased with the human race.*

PROVERBS 8:30-31, GNT

CHAPTER 3

THE HAPPINESS-KILLERS

HOW DOES SIN AFFECT OUR HAPPINESS?

We often allow sin to thwart our happiness by going where we shouldn't. God instructs us,

> *Do not enter the path of the wicked, and do not walk in the way of the evil. Avoid it; do not go on it; turn away from it and pass on.*

PROVERBS 4:14-15

Our Creator lovingly warns us that sin is utterly disastrous. Disobeying God never brings happiness. Its fruit is death, self-destruction, loss, and disgrace (see Proverbs 1:31-33; 2:19, 22; 3:35). Satan tells us one thing; God, another. But human experience only vindicates God's claims. If we comparison shop between sin and Jesus, the difference is obvious. Sin brings misery; Jesus brings happiness. Which will you choose?

Of course, there are "fleeting pleasures of sin" (Hebrews 11:25). An injection of heroin or an immoral act can bring moments of pleasure—but not deep and lasting happiness. Sin can for the short term *make* us happy, but it won't *leave* us happy.

Sin is the biggest enemy of happiness because it results in a broken relationship with God. Forgiveness is its greatest friend, because it reunites us with the happy God.

> *We ourselves were once foolish, disobedient, led astray, slaves to various passions and pleasures, passing our days in malice and envy, hated by others and hating one another. But when the goodness and loving kindness of God our Savior appeared, he saved us, not because of works done by us in righteousness, but according to his own mercy, by the washing of regeneration and renewal of the Holy Spirit.*

TITUS 3:3-5

HOW CAN WE STOP FEELING GUILTY AND BE HAPPY INSTEAD?

Confession of sin brings happiness. Someone who puts his hand in a fire feels excruciating pain, causing him to withdraw it and seek medical attention. *He's far better off because of the pain.*

In contrast, someone with leprosy, who feels nothing because of damaged nerve endings, might *seem* happier for not experiencing the agony. But he'll suffer long term because his body still experiences destruction, whether or not he realizes it.

This world desensitizes us to evil, turning us into moral lepers who become numb to healthy twinges of conscience.

Charles Spurgeon said, "It does not spoil your happiness . . . to confess your sin. The unhappiness is in not making the confession."[21]

Happiness is impossible without repentance, forgiveness, and a right relationship with Christ. It's like trying to turn on a light that's unplugged. Darkness remains.

- Whoever conceals his transgressions will not prosper, but he who confesses and forsakes them will obtain mercy. (Proverbs 28:13)

- If while we were enemies we were reconciled to God by the death of his Son, much more, now that we are reconciled, shall we be saved by his life. (Romans 5:10)

WHAT MAKES WORRY THE ENEMY OF HAPPINESS?
Montaigne said something that rings true for many of us: "My life has been full of terrible misfortunes, most of which never happened."[22]

Worry is a killjoy. God tells his children there's much to rejoice about:

1. He's already rescued us from the worst—eternal Hell.
2. Even if something terrible happens, he'll use it for our eternal good.
3. Often bad things don't happen, and our worry proves groundless.
4. Whether or not bad things happen, our worry accomplishes nothing.
5. The cause for all our worries—sin and the Curse—is temporary and will soon be behind us. Forever.

Just after instructing us to rejoice in the Lord, Paul writes,

> *Don't worry about anything; instead, pray about everything. Tell God what you need, and thank him for all he has done. Then you will experience God's peace, which exceeds anything we can understand. His peace will guard your hearts and minds as you live in Christ Jesus.*
>
> PHILIPPIANS 4:6-7, NLT

Instead of worrying, we're to thank God for his promise to work everything together for good, trusting in his sovereign grace:

> *We know that for those who love God all things work together for good, for those who are called according to his purpose.*
>
> ROMANS 8:28

HOW DOES AN ENTITLEMENT MENTALITY AFFECT HAPPINESS?

Nothing is more poisonous than the spirit of entitlement that permeates our culture and sometimes, sadly, our churches. Some people are perpetually disappointed with their employer, their employees, the waiter, the salesclerk, the coach, the referee, the airline, the government, the police, family, friends, neighbors, and church. This robs us of happiness and God of glory.

If we believe God's in charge, then our complaints are about him. How dare he not give us what we want, when we want it?

We should see things as they are. We deserve expulsion; God gives us a diploma. We deserve the electric chair; he gives us a parade. Anything less than overwhelming gratitude should be unthinkable. He owes us *nothing*. We owe him *everything*.

A "Dear Abby" letter read, "Happiness is having parents that trust you. Happiness is getting the telephone call you've been praying for. Happiness is knowing that you're well dressed as anybody. Happiness is something I don't have. Signed, Fifteen and Unhappy."[23]

A few days later, the same column carried this response, written by a thirteen-year-old girl: "Happiness is being able to walk. Happiness is being able to talk. Happiness is being able to see.

Happiness is being able to hear. Unhappiness is reading a letter from a 15-year-old girl who can do all these things and still says she isn't happy. I can talk, I can see, I can hear, but I can't walk. Signed, Thirteen and Happy."[24]

The happiest people in the world are those who have a deep, gratitude-drenched relationship with Christ. There is no place for Christian curmudgeons.

> *Do all things without grumbling or disputing,*
> *that you may be blameless and innocent,*
> *children of God without blemish in the midst*
> *of a crooked and twisted generation, among*
> *whom you shine as lights in the world.*

PHILIPPIANS 2:14-15

HOW CAN WE FIND HAPPINESS . . . OR REGAIN THE HAPPINESS WE'VE LOST?

To be happy in God, we must believe and meditate daily on what's true about him.

Psalm 37:4 reads, "Delight *yourself* in the LORD" (emphasis added). We aren't spoon-fed his pleasures while doing nothing. We need to go to his banquet, reach out our hands, and delight ourselves with that delicious cuisine. As surely as it's our responsibility to put good food in our mouths, it's our responsibility to be happy in God and cultivate our appetite for him!

God says we are to long for his Word as newborn babies long for milk "now that you have had a taste of the Lord's kindness" (1 Peter 2:3, NLT). We should contemplate God's great works in the natural world and ponder his incomparable redemptive work for us—then gratefully praise him for his goodness. This makes him *and* us happy!

- May the righteous be glad and rejoice before God; may they be happy and joyful. (Psalm 68:3, NIV)
- Seek the Kingdom of God above all else, and live righteously, and he will give you everything you need. (Matthew 6:33, NLT)

WHAT DOES HOLINESS HAVE TO DO WITH HAPPINESS?
I talked with a young woman who knew that following Christ was the right thing to do but thought it required sacrificing her happiness.

Unless her view changes dramatically, her spiritual future is bleak. It isn't in our nature to continually say no to what we believe would make us happy—or yes to what would make us unhappy.

Christians see the world seeking happiness instead of holiness, so we assume we should not seek happiness at all. But this false contrast between holiness and happiness is both unbiblical and impractical. The devil's lie is that embracing holiness brings unhappiness. But God says duty and delight are connected.

Despite the fact that ancient Israel faced near-constant threats of enemy attack, a new husband was exempt from military service. God said, "He shall be free at home one year to be *happy* with his wife" (Deuteronomy 24:5, emphasis added). The verb used here is causative, meaning not merely "to *be* happy" but "to *make* happy." In many people's minds, duty and happiness are contradictory, but God commands the young husband to experience happiness with his wife!

Scripture directly links happiness and holiness: "May your holy people be happy because of your goodness" (2 Chronicles 6:41, NCV). To be holy is to see God as he is and to become like him, covered in Christ's righteousness. Since God's nature is to be happy, the more like him we become, the happier we become.

- Let your priests be clothed with righteousness, and let your saints shout for joy. (Psalm 132:9)
- Happy and holy is the one who shares in the first resurrection! (Revelation 20:6, PHILLIPS)

CHAPTER 4

LOOKING FOR HAPPINESS IN ALL THE RIGHT PLACES

IS IT OKAY FOR CHRISTIANS TO PARTY?

Partying is rarely associated with the Bible and Christ-followers . . . but it *should* be! The Bible's many references to singing, dancing, celebrations, feasts, and festivities depict not only worship but fun, laughter, and pleasure.

Part of what blinds us to God's emphasis on happiness is our awareness that pagans worshiped pleasure deities and their celebrations centered on drunkenness and immorality.

Partying suffers from guilt by association. The logic goes like this: since immorality is bad, sex is bad. Since drunkenness is bad, alcohol is bad. Since laziness is bad, rest is bad. Since greed is bad, money is bad. Since gluttony is bad, food is bad. But in fact, the abuse of a good thing doesn't make it a bad thing! Partying is God honoring when God and his good gifts are celebrated.

- Spend the money for whatever you desire—oxen or sheep or wine or strong drink, whatever your appetite craves. And you shall eat there before the LORD your God and rejoice, you and your household. (Deuteronomy 14:26)
- Nehemiah continued, "Go and celebrate with a feast of rich foods and sweet drinks, and share gifts of food with people who have nothing prepared. This is a sacred day before our Lord. Don't be dejected and sad, for the joy of the LORD is your strength!" (Nehemiah 8:10, NLT)
- You are the LORD's people! So celebrate and praise the only God. (Psalm 97:12, CEV)

WHAT STEPS CAN WE TAKE TO BECOME HAPPIER?
First and foremost, by God's grace, embrace Christ's work on the cross to pay for your sins and reconcile you to God (see 2 Corinthians 5:18-20). What

could be more happy-making than knowing the God of happiness, who grants us eternal life and happiness in Christ?

Sonja Lyubomirsky, one of the world's foremost experts on happiness, admits, "I don't have a religious or spiritual bone in my body." Yet she acknowledges that studies clearly show that people with faith in God are happier.[25] In contrast, a naturalistic worldview that affirms randomness and meaninglessness doesn't lend itself to happiness. Those with such beliefs often illogically borrow from the Christian worldview in order to have a sense of purpose and fulfillment.

Once we've been reconciled to God, we can do something more about our happiness by *doing what happy people do*. Happiness doesn't precede giving and serving; it *accompanies* and *follows* it.

Insanity is doing the same things over and over while expecting different results. If we want new and better results when it comes to our happiness, we must step out and do something different! If you're unhappy, you need to change what you're thinking *and* what you're doing.

- I have always shown you that you must work hard, as I have. You must help those who cannot work. By so doing you are remembering the words of the Lord Jesus. He said, "It makes you more happy to give something than to get something." (Acts 20:35, WE)
- Let us use [our spiritual gifts] . . . the one who does acts of mercy, with cheerfulness. (Romans 12:6, 8)

HOW CAN WE BE HAPPY IN THE MIDST OF DIFFICULT CIRCUMSTANCES?

Countless people in worse situations are happier than those in better situations. This demonstrates that happiness is dependent not on circumstances but on perspective, which is determined by our focus.

David Brainerd was orphaned at fourteen and suffered from debilitating tuberculosis. One day he "found some relief in prayer; loved, as a feeble, afflicted, despised creature, to cast myself on a God of infinite grace and goodness, hoping for no happiness but from Him. . . . Toward night, I felt

my soul rejoice that God is unchangeably happy
and glorious."[26]

Brainerd made the daily choice to connect
with God's Word and God's people and to behold
him in his creation. This is never easy in debilitating circumstances, but God has promised to
give us strength to persevere as we trust him. If a
young man dying of an excruciating disease, in a
culture without modern painkillers, could make
choices that brought him happiness in Christ,
surely we can too.

- I concluded there is nothing better than to
  be happy and enjoy ourselves as long as we
  can. (Ecclesiastes 3:12, NLT)
- [God's] divine power has granted to us all
  things that pertain to life and godliness,
  through the knowledge of him who called us
  to his own glory and excellence. (2 Peter 1:3)

HOW CAN READING THE BIBLE INCREASE
OUR HAPPINESS?

Happiness among believers is proportionate to
the time invested in the humble study of God's

Word. There's nothing wrong with learning about sports and politics. But only God's Word prepares us to live wisely and to die well.

Joni Eareckson Tada says, "Great faith . . . [is] simply taking God at his word and taking the next step."[27] Just as we can't follow signs without getting on the road, we can't take God at his Word unless we spend time reading, hearing, and contemplating it.

Through Scripture meditation, prayer, group Bible study, and sitting under the teaching of God's Word, we get to know our Lord better and draw closer to him. In the process, we cultivate overflowing happiness.

Jesus said, "My sheep hear my voice, and I know them, and they follow me" (John 10:27). People are unhappy because they listen to the thousands of unhappy voices—including much media—that clamor for their attention. Joy comes from hearing and believing words from the Source of joy.

- The laws of the LORD are true; each one is fair. They are more desirable than gold, even the finest gold. They are sweeter

than honey, even honey dripping from the
comb. (Psalm 19:9-10, NLT)

- As your words came to me I drank them
  in, and they filled my heart with joy
  and happiness because I belong to you,
  O LORD, the God who rules over all.
  (Jeremiah 15:16, NET)

SOME SAY, "SEEK THE GIVER, NOT THE GIFT"; DOES THIS MEAN GOD'S GIFTS SHOULDN'T MAKE US HAPPY?

It's better to say, "Seek the giver *through* the gift."
We should appreciate and enjoy a wonderful
meal, aware that its pleasure is God's gift to us.
By enjoying it, we're enjoying him.

Jesus said, "If you then, who are evil, know
how to give good gifts to your children, how much
more will your Father who is in heaven give good
things to those who ask him!" (Matthew 7:11).

God himself is our greatest gift. As long as we
see God in his gifts to us, we need not fear we're
appreciating them too much. John Calvin wrote,
"In despising the gifts, we insult the Giver."[28]

Idolatry becomes a threat whenever we divorce God from pleasure and happiness, whereas if we accept God's invitation to taste and enjoy delicious food, then we can welcome God's invitation to "taste and see that the LORD is good" (Psalm 34:8). That's a directive to go to God and experience pleasure and happiness in him! The God who wants us to take pleasure in him made a world filled with pleasures pointing us to him.

- You prepare a feast for me in the presence of my enemies. You honor me by anointing my head with oil. My cup overflows with blessings. (Psalm 23:5, NLT)
- Every good gift and every perfect gift is from above, coming down from the Father of lights. (James 1:17)

IS IT SELFISH TO WANT HAPPINESS?

Many Christians believe that desiring happiness is selfish and therefore immoral. Why? Partly because we fail to balance biblical statements with one another.

The Bible warns against those who are "lovers

of self," identifying them as boastful, proud, and unholy (see 2 Timothy 3:2). The self-love spoken of in this passage is obviously wrong. However, when Jesus tells us to love our neighbors as ourselves, he isn't arguing that we shouldn't love ourselves but that we should instead extend our instincts for self-care to taking care of others.

Flight crews routinely announce, "If you're traveling with a child or someone who requires assistance, in the case of an emergency, secure your own oxygen mask first before helping the other person." It may sound selfish to put on our own masks, just as it sounds selfish to say that one of our main duties in life is to find happiness in God. But only then are we in a position to offer others what they most need.

> *[Jesus] said to him, "You shall love the Lord your God with all your heart and with all your soul and with all your mind. This is the great and first commandment. And a second is like it: You shall love your neighbor as yourself."*
>
> MATTHEW 22:37-39

HOW CAN SELF-FORGETFULNESS ENHANCE OUR HAPPINESS?

When I meditate on Christ's unfathomable love and grace, I lose myself in him, and before I know it, I'm happy. But when I focus on my problems and especially how badly others are treating me (or so I imagine), happiness flies away.

C. S. Lewis said of the humble person, "He will not be thinking about humility: he will not be thinking about himself at all."[29]

Tim Keller says, "Gospel-humility is not needing to think about myself. . . . I stop connecting every experience, every conversation, with myself. . . . The freedom of self-forgetfulness."[30]

When we lose ourselves in God's purposes, Jesus says we'll find ourselves—and also happiness. The "sacrifice" of following Jesus produces in us the greatest, most lasting happiness.

- Whoever finds his life will lose it, and whoever loses his life for my sake will find it. (Matthew 10:39)
- Rejoice always, pray without ceasing, in everything give thanks. (1 Thessalonians 5:16-18, NKJV)

HOW CAN BEING GRATEFUL INCREASE OUR HAPPINESS?

If we truly grasped even a little of God's grace, we'd fall on our knees and weep. Then we'd get up and dance, smile, laugh, look at each other, and say, "Can you *believe* it? We're forgiven!"

God isn't just in life's monumental moments. He's present in raindrops, the artistry of spiderwebs, the sound of an acoustic guitar, a child's laugh, a swing set, sprinklers, the smell of split cedar, the taste of maple syrup, and a dog's wagging tail. If we disregard these and thousands of other gifts, we don't just fail to notice them, *we fail to notice God.*

God gives us hundreds of reasons to be grateful every hour—and if you think I'm exaggerating, ask him to open your eyes to his gracious provisions surrounding you. Developing the habit of gratitude results in greater praise to God and greater happiness for ourselves.

Consider taking a "thankfulness walk" daily in which you ponder God's goodness in your life and praise him for his gifts. If you're unable to walk, ponder God's kindness in sustaining your mind and giving you food to eat and air to breathe.

Someone asked a man why he was so happy. He picked up a binder filled with hundreds of handwritten pages. "Every time someone does something kind for me or I feel good about something, I write it in this book. I've learned to see and remember and be grateful for kindness and happiness when they come."

- Let them sacrifice thank offerings and tell of his works with songs of joy. (Psalm 107:22, NIV)
- Look at the lilies of the field and how they grow. They don't work or make their clothing, yet Solomon in all his glory was not dressed as beautifully as they are. (Matthew 6:28-29, NLT)

WHY IS IT IMPORTANT TO DEVELOP A CONSCIOUSNESS OF GOD'S PRESENCE IN AND AROUND US EACH DAY?
Alexander Maclaren advised, "Seek . . . to cultivate a buoyant, joyous sense of the crowded kindnesses of God in your daily life."[31] If we fail to see God's "crowded kindnesses," it's because we're blind to them.

C. S. Lewis said of God, "The world is crowded with Him. He walks everywhere incognito."[32] Lewis spoke of God's self-revelation through his creation: "Any patch of sunlight in a wood will show you something about the sun which you could never get from reading books on astronomy. These pure and spontaneous pleasures are 'patches of Godlight' in the woods of our experience."[33]

Some believe it only matters that we see God in the big things. Lewis disagreed, saying, "We—or at least I—shall not be able to adore God on the highest occasions if we have learned no habit of doing so on the lowest."[34]

- Since the creation of the world God's invisible qualities—his eternal power and divine nature—have been clearly seen. (Romans 1:20, NIV)

- Though you have not seen him, you love him. Though you do not now see him, you believe in him and rejoice with joy that is inexpressible and filled with glory. (1 Peter 1:8)

CHAPTER 5

GOOD NEWS OF HAPPINESS TODAY, TOMORROW, AND FOREVER

HOW CAN WE USE THE PURSUIT OF HAPPINESS TO SPREAD THE GOSPEL?

If the gospel doesn't make us happy, we're not believing the Good News or grasping its extent. We need to remind ourselves of what the gospel really means. As Jerry Bridges says, "Preach the gospel to yourself every day."[35]

If only the church today would grasp what God's people have always known and embrace happiness-seeking as an ally in preaching the Good News!

If someone expresses a desire to be happy, we should never say, "That's selfish; you just need to obey God" but rather, "God wired you that way."

Then we can ask, "Have the things you thought would make you happy been successful?" The answer is probably no. That's the time to suggest, "Maybe you haven't looked in the right place."

We can first present the Bible's bad news about the Fall and sin and the Curse, which explains why the person is unhappy. Then we can share the good news about Jesus' life, death, and resurrection, and the opportunity to believe in him, become right with God, and gain assurance of eternal happiness.

- The people were full of *joy* because God had made them very *happy*. (Nehemiah 12:43, GNT)
- Rejoice in the LORD and be *happy*, you who are godly! Shout for *joy*. (Psalm 32:11, NET)

WHAT'S SO GOOD ABOUT THE GOOD NEWS?

The angel said to the shepherds at the birth of Jesus, "I bring you good news of great joy that will be for all the people" (Luke 2:10).

The gospel isn't just for some; it's for all. The Greek adjective translated "great" here is *megas*— good news of "mega-joy"!

If you've ever wondered whether God loves you,

listen to Scripture: "God showed how much he loved us by sending his one and only Son into the world so that we might have eternal life through him. This is real love" (1 John 4:9-10, NLT).

We're told of the wise men concerning the star of Bethlehem, "When they saw it, how happy they were, what joy was theirs!" (Matthew 2:9-10, GNT).

Imagine how people might respond if we emphasized that Jesus' death on the cross was for the sake of never-ending happiness—ours and his. We'd be proclaiming an aspect of the gospel that's not only exceedingly attractive but also entirely true. The gospel offers an exchange of misery-generating sin for happiness-giving righteousness provided by Jesus. That's an incredible bargain—and startlingly good news!

- Do not rejoice in this, that the spirits are subject to you, but rejoice that your names are written in heaven. (Luke 10:20)
- For God so loved the world, that he gave his only Son, that whoever believes in him should not perish but have eternal life. (John 3:16)

HOW IMPORTANT TO OUR HAPPINESS IS GOD'S FORGIVENESS?

David described forgiveness this way: "Happy are those to whom the LORD imputes no iniquity, and in whose spirit there is no deceit" (Psalm 32:2, NRSV).

He then recounted his state of utter misery after his adultery with Bathsheba and the murder of her husband, Uriah: "While I kept silence, my body wasted away through my groaning all day long. . . . My strength was dried up as by the heat of summer" (Psalm 32:3-4, NRSV).

David chose the sin of adultery to find happiness, and subsequent murder to cover up his sin *so he could be happy.* Yet both sins brought extreme *unhappiness.*

His confession changed everything:

> *I acknowledged my sin to you, and I did not hide my iniquity; I said, "I will confess my transgressions to the LORD," and you forgave the guilt of my sin. . . . You surround me with glad cries of deliverance.*

PSALM 32:5, 7, NRSV

David began Psalm 32 with "Happy is . . ." and ended with "Rejoice and be happy in the LORD" (verse 11, NCV).

When sin is removed, misery is lifted. There's only one way to be at peace with God so his happiness flows freely to us:

> *If we confess our sins, he is faithful and just to forgive us our sins and to cleanse us from all unrighteousness.*
>
> I JOHN 1:9

HOW CENTRAL TO OUR HAPPINESS IS OUR CLOSENESS TO JESUS?

Jesus said to people starving for peace, hope, significance, and happiness, "I am the bread of life; whoever comes to me shall not hunger, and whoever believes in me shall never thirst" (John 6:35).

Jesus cried out, "If anyone thirsts, let him come to me and drink. Whoever believes in me, as the Scripture has said, 'Out of his heart will flow rivers of living water'" (John 7:37-38).

Christ quenches our thirst from the inside. His Holy Spirit indwells us so whatever heartbreaking circumstances we face, rivers of life-giving water will flow from our hearts.

When Jesus says, "I am the way, and the truth, and the life. No one comes to the Father except through me" (John 14:6), he's also saying, "I am the only way to the Father's happiness."

Peter preached that Jesus was "full of gladness" (Acts 2:28). Jesus offers us more than happiness— but certainly nothing less.

- These things I have spoken to you, that my joy may be in you, and that your joy may be full. (John 15:11)
- Now I come to You; and these things I speak in the world so that they may have My joy made full in themselves. (John 17:13, NASB)

HOW DOES OUR UNDERSTANDING OF THE RESURRECTION AND NEW EARTH AFFECT OUR PRESENT HAPPINESS?

A character in the movie *Pirate Radio* says, "You know, a few months ago, I made a terrible mistake. . . . Instead of crushing the thought the moment it came . . . I'm afraid it's stuck in my head forever. These are the best days of our lives. It's a terrible thing to know, but I know it."[36]

This fictional character is absolutely right: for people with no faith in God, these *are* the best days, and tragically they're winding down to a permanent end.

But for genuine Christ-followers, the best by far is yet to come! J. I. Packer puts it well: "Hearts on earth say in the course of a joyful experience, 'I don't want this ever to end.' But it invariably does. The hearts of those in heaven say, 'I want this to go on forever.' And it will. There can be no better news than this."[37]

Jesus told his disciples of a coming new world, "the renewal of all things, when the Son of Man sits on his glorious throne" (Matthew 19:28, NIV). Scripture beautifully portrays what awaits God's children:

I saw a new heaven and a new earth. . . . I saw the holy city, new Jerusalem, coming down out of heaven from God. . . . And I heard a loud voice from the throne saying,

"Behold, the dwelling place of God is with man. He will dwell with them, and they will be his people, and God himself will be with them as their God. He will wipe away every tear from their eyes, and death shall be no more, neither shall there be mourning, nor crying, nor pain anymore, for the former things have passed away."

REVELATION 21:1-4

We normally think of going up to Heaven to live with God in his place. That's what happens when believers die. But the ultimate promise is that *God will come down to live with us in our place*, on the New Earth. The ultimate Heaven will not be "us with God" but "God with us" (see Revelation 21:3).

We'll be physical beings living in a physical world—eating, drinking, playing, working, and laughing to God's glory. That's the promise of the Resurrection—eternal delight and joy in the presence of our Redeemer. Peter preached in Jerusalem of "the final restoration of all things, as God promised long ago through his holy prophets" (Acts 3:21, NLT).

A. W. Tozer wrote, "When the followers of Jesus Christ lose their interest in heaven they will no longer be happy Christians, and when they are no longer happy Christians they cannot be a powerful force in a sad and sinful world."[38]

It's tragic for Christ-followers to think the only place we can experience what's good is here and now. Sin, the Fall, and the Curse are *not* the norm for the created universe; they're temporary aberrations that Christ will decisively destroy and permanently replace with a New Heaven and New Earth.

The typical view of Heaven—eternity in a disembodied state—is not only completely contrary to Scripture but obscures the far richer truth: God promises us eternal life as healthy, embodied people who've said a final good-bye to sin and suffering and are *more* capable of worship, friendship, love, discovery, work, play, and *happiness* than we've ever been.

- We fix our eyes not on what is seen, but on what is unseen, since what is seen is temporary, but what is unseen is eternal. (2 Corinthians 4:18, NIV)

- We will be with the Lord forever. . . .
  Encourage one another with these words.
  (1 Thessalonians 4:17-18, NIV)

SHOULD WE WORRY ABOUT BEING PAST OUR PEAKS?

All who know Jesus will live together in that resurrected world, with the Lord we love and the friends we cherish. Jesus will be the center of everything. Happiness will be our lifeblood. And just when we think, *It doesn't get any better than this* . . . it will!

Millions of years from now, in the presence of the happy God who will never tire of us, we'll daily be able to say, "I'll never be separated from my endlessly loving and creative God and Savior, the Source of all happiness. Every day has been better than the one before . . . and the best is yet to be!"

Knowing that the best is not behind us but before us should radically affect our view of aging and deteriorating health. We don't look back wistfully to when we were at our peaks; we look forward to the day when we will experience new peaks we never got close to in this world.

If you or your loved one is dying, rejoice that one day all who know Jesus will have bodies and minds far better than the best we've ever known. We'll think and act in ways that will amaze us—unhindered by sin and suffering.

If you know Jesus, don't worry about a bucket list, since you'll live forever in a redeemed body on a redeemed earth, where the adventures will be far greater than now. Enjoy good memories. But don't spend your remaining days here looking back, wishing for "the good old days." Instead, look forward to "the great new days"! Meanwhile, trust God for strength for today's challenges.

- O death, where is your victory? O death, where is your sting? (1 Corinthians 15:55)
- The Lord Jesus Christ . . . will transform our lowly bodies so that they will be like his glorious body. (Philippians 3:20-21, NIV)

WHAT WILL HAPPINESS BE LIKE ON THE NEW EARTH?
God's original plan included human beings living happy and fulfilled lives. Imagine sitting around campfires on the New Earth, wide eyed

at adventures recounted. Yes, I mean telling real stories around real campfires. After all, friendship, camaraderie, laughter, stories, and campfires are gifts from God for physical people living in a physical world . . . and that's precisely who and where we will be forever!

We're told "his servants will serve him" (Revelation 22:3, NIV). That means we'll be doing meaningful and no doubt creative work for Jesus. And we'll enjoy rest and relaxation (see Hebrews 4:1-11; Revelation 14:13).

Will we eat and drink as resurrected beings? Scripture couldn't be more emphatic on this point (see Matthew 8:11; Revelation 2:7; 19:9). Jesus said, "People will come from east and west, and from north and south, and recline at table in the kingdom of God" (Luke 13:29).

Isaiah 25:6 says, "On this mountain the LORD of hosts will make for all peoples a feast of rich food, a feast of well-aged wine." How good a meal will *that* be?

Heaven will be deeply appreciated by the disabled, who'll be liberated from ravaged bodies and minds, and the sick and the elderly, who'll be free from pains and restrictions. They'll walk, run, see, and hear—some for the first time.

Father Boudreaux envisioned the eternal reunion of God's people: "What outbursts of gladness among the members of his family! . . . Death shall be no more, and therefore we shall never more be torn away from the society of our kindred and friends."[39]

Picture Jesus approaching, with a smile on his face, as we're laughing, playing, talking, and reminiscing with friends and family on the redeemed Earth. We all fall to our knees in worship. He pulls us up and embraces us. What happiness!

- The cow will graze near the bear. The cub and the calf will lie down together. The lion will eat hay like a cow. The baby will play safely near the hole of a cobra. Yes, a little child will put its hand in a nest of deadly snakes without harm. Nothing will hurt or destroy in all my holy mountain, for as the waters fill the sea, so the earth will be filled with people who know the LORD. In that day the heir to David's throne will be a banner of salvation to all the world. The nations will rally to him, and the land where he lives will be a glorious place. (Isaiah 11:7-10, NLT)

- The streets of the city shall be full of boys and girls playing. (Zechariah 8:5)
- We are looking forward to the new heavens and new earth he has promised, a world filled with God's righteousness. (2 Peter 3:13, NLT)

HAPPINESS IS THE PROPER RESPONSE TO GOOD NEWS

When you speak of heaven, let your face light up with a heavenly gleam. Let your eyes shine with reflected glory. And when you speak of hell— well, then your usual face will do.

CHARLES SPURGEON, TO A CLASS OF SEMINARY STUDENTS

When we hear good news, what's our reaction? Happiness, excitement, delight, and celebration, right? The greater the news, the greater the happiness.

The Good News is a concrete, reality-grounded call to happiness: Jesus really did become a man, go to the cross, and rise from the grave. He truly is with us now and will return one day. These facts separate the gospel from wishful thinking.

God is a promise keeper, not a promise breaker. He promises his children eternal happiness, saying he'll live with us on the New Earth forever. After promising no more death, suffering, crying, or pain (see Revelation 21:1, 3-4), Jesus instructs the apostle John, "Write this down, for these words are trustworthy and true" (21:5). These are the words of the King. Count on them.

But while we're promised eternal happiness, Christ doesn't want us to wait until we die to experience happiness. Jesus says, "I came that they may have life and have it abundantly" (John 10:10). The word translated "abundantly" suggests something profuse in quantity and quality—a surpassingly happy life. Similarly, Scripture describes a full, satisfying life: "God gave us eternal life, and this life is in his Son" (1 John 5:11). The phrase "eternal life" appears forty-three times in the New Testament. It means far more than living forever—*it means being happy forever*!

John says he wrote his gospel "that you may believe that Jesus is the Messiah, the Son of God, and that by believing you may have life in his

name" (John 20:31, NIV). We don't have to won-
der whether we have eternal life: "I write these
things to you who believe in the name of the Son
of God that you may know that you have eternal
life" (1 John 5:13).

The gospel infuses hope and joy into our
current circumstances by acknowledging God's
greatness over any crisis we'll face. God is for us,
and not even death can separate us from God's
love (see Romans 8:31-39). If we really believe
these truths, how can we not be happy?

Fred Sanders writes, "A gospel which is only
about the moment of conversion but does not
extend to every moment of life in Christ is too
small. A gospel that gets your sins forgiven but
offers no power for transformation is too small."[40]
And a gospel incapable of making you happier
than you've ever been is also too small.

The gospel is very much about happiness.
Delivery from eternal damnation is delivery from
eternal misery. What better qualifies as the "good
news of happiness" (Isaiah 52:7)? What better
sums up God's gifts of goodness, loving-kindness,
grace, mercy, salvation, rebirth, renewal, and the

indwelling Holy Spirit (see Titus 3:5-7) than the word *happiness*?

Those who trust and serve Christ receive this mind-boggling invitation: "Come and share your master's happiness!" (Matthew 25:21, NIV). Those who trust anything and anyone other than Christ to meet their deepest needs are told, "Weep and howl for the miseries that are coming upon you" (James 5:1).

As a young believer, I often heard testimonies in which people happily recalled the day of their conversion. Years later, I realized that I should be happy not just for what God has done in the past or will do in the future, but for what he's doing *today*. The psalmist spoke of a particular day when he said, "This is the day that the LORD has made; let us rejoice and be glad in it" (Psalm 118:24). But God has made every single day of our lives and has a reason for them all (see Psalm 139:16). We're to find joy in each of them (see Philippians 4:4).

What if we spread the extraordinarily good news of Jesus by offering people the happiness they long for? Imagine if churches were known for being communities of Jesus-centered happiness, overflowing with the sheer gladness of what it means to live out the Good News!

If God's happiness is truly permeating his people, make no mistake: our children, grandchildren, and communities will know it. Seeing God's happiness overflow from his people will be far more attractive to the happiness-seeking world. Some will realize, *Maybe those people have found the happiness I crave.* And they will listen with interest to the good news of happiness in Jesus.

Meanwhile, won't we experience far more gladness by living lives not merely pushed by duty but pulled by delight in Jesus?

> *[Jesus said,] "How happy are you who weep now, for you are going to laugh!"*
> LUKE 6:21, PHILLIPS

NOTES

1. Thomas A. Hand, *St. Augustine on Prayer* (South Bend, IN: Newman Press, 1963), 1.

2. Blaise Pascal, *Pensées*, number 425.

3. Thomas Manton, "Twenty Sermons on Important Passages of Scripture," *The Complete Works of Thomas Manton*, vol. 2.

4. J. C. Ryle, *Happiness: The Secret of Happiness as Found in the Bible* (Cedar Lake, MI: Waymark Books, 2011), 7.

5. A. W. Tozer, *Who Put Jesus on the Cross?* (Camp Hill, PA: WingSpread, 2009), e-book.

6. *Merriam-Webster Unabridged Dictionary* (Britannica Digital Learning, 2014), s.v. "joy," http://www.merriam-webster.com/dictionary/joy.

7. John Piper, "Let Your Passion Be Single," Desiring God, November 12, 1999, http://www.desiringgod.org/conference-messages/let-your-passion-be-single.

8. Joni Eareckson Tada, *Joni and Friends Daily Devotional*, November 28, 2013.

9. Therese J. Borchard, "How Giving Makes Us Happy," *World of Psychology* (blog), PsychCentral.com, December 22, 2013, http://psychcentral.com/blog/archives/2013/12/22/how-giving-makes-us-happy/.

10. Gavin Andrews and Scott Henderson, eds., *Unmet Need in Psychiatry: Problems, Resources, Responses* (Cambridge: Cambridge University Press, 2000), 239.

11. Dennis Prager, *Happiness Is a Serious Problem: A Human Nature Repair Manual* (New York: ReganBooks, 1998), 115.

12. David Murray, "7 Kinds of Happiness," *HeadHeartHand* (blog), September 17, 2014, http://headhearthand.org/blog/2014/09/17/7-types-of-happiness/.

13. C. S. Lewis, *Mere Christianity* (New York: HarperCollins, 2001), book 2, chapter 3, "The Shocking Alternative."

14. John Phillips, *Exploring the Pastoral Epistles: An Expository Commentary* (Grand Rapids, MI: Kregel, 2004), 190.

15. Robert Jamieson, A. R. Fausset, and David Brown, *Commentary Critical and Explanatory on the Whole Bible*, 1 Timothy 1:11.

16. Noah Webster, *An American Dictionary of the English Language*, vol. 1 (New York: S. Converse, 1828), 273.

17. Charles H. Spurgeon, "Adorning the Gospel" (Sermon #2416).

18. Jonathan Edwards, in John Piper, "Undoing the Destruction of Pleasure," Desiring God, April 10, 2001, http://www.desiringgod.org/conference-messages/undoing-the-destruction-of-pleasure.

19. John Piper, "Is Jesus an Egomaniac?" Desiring God, January 4, 2010, http://www.desiringgod.org/conference-messages /is-jesus-an-egomaniac.

20. A. W. Tozer, *The Attributes of God*, vol. 1 (Camp Hill, PA: WingSpread, 2007), 10, 12–13.

21. Charles H. Spurgeon, "Sorrow and Sorrow" (Sermon #2691).

22. Michel de Montaigne, as quoted in Paul McKenna, *Change Your Life in Seven Days* (London: Transworld, 2004), 159.

23. Charles Allen McClain, *Good News for Off Seasons* (Nashville: Abingdon Press, 1979), 49.

24. Ibid.

25. Sonja Lyubomirsky, "Happiness and Religion, Happiness as Religion," *How of Happiness* (blog), *Psychology Today*, June 25, 2008, 234, http://www.psychologytoday.com/blog /how-happiness/200806/happiness-and-religion-happiness -religion.

26. David Brainerd, as quoted in Jonathan Edwards, *Life and Diary of David Brainerd* (New York: Cosimo, 2007), 153, 183.

27. Joni Eareckson Tada, as quoted by Gladys Haynes Green, *God's Faithfulness: The Greens' Journey* (Bloomington, IN: CrossBooks, 2012), 74.

28. John Calvin, *Institutes of the Christian Religion*, trans. Henry Beveridge, Book Second, chapter 2, "Man Now Deprived of Freedom of Will, and Miserably Enslaved."

29. Lewis, *Mere Christianity*, book 3, chapter 8, "The Great Sin."

30. Timothy Keller, *The Freedom of Self-Forgetfulness* (Denver: 10Publishing, 2012), 32.

31. Alexander Maclaren, "Requiting God," *Expositions of Holy Scripture: Psalms.*

32. C. S. Lewis, *Letters to Malcolm* (New York: Harcourt, 2002), 75.

33. Ibid., 91.

34. Ibid.

35. Jerry Bridges, *Respectable Sins: Confronting the Sins We Tolerate* (Colorado Springs: NavPress, 2007), 36.

36. *Pirate Radio*, directed by Richard Curtis (Universal Studios, 2009).

37. J. I. Packer, *Concise Theology* (Carol Stream, IL: Tyndale, 1993), 267.

38 A. W. Tozer and H. Verploegh, *The Quotable Tozer II: More Wise Words with a Prophetic Edge* (Camp Hill, PA: Christian Publications, 1997), 103–104.

39. F. J. Boudreaux, *The Happiness of Heaven*, chapter 11.

40. Fred Sanders, *The Deep Things of God: How the Trinity Changes Everything* (Wheaton, IL: Crossway, 2010), 106.

ABOUT THE AUTHOR

RANDY ALCORN is an author and the founder and director of Eternal Perspective Ministries (EPM), a nonprofit organization dedicated to teaching principles of God's Word and assisting the church in ministering to unreached, unfed, unborn, uneducated, unreconciled, and unsupported people around the world. His ministry focus is communicating the strategic importance of using our earthly time, money, possessions, and opportunities to invest in need-meeting ministries that count for eternity. He accomplishes this by analyzing, teaching, and applying biblical truth.

Before starting EPM in 1990, Randy served as a pastor for fourteen years. He has a bachelor of theology and a master of arts in biblical studies from Multnomah University and an honorary doctorate from Western Seminary in Portland, Oregon, and has taught on the adjunct faculties of both. A *New York Times* bestselling author, Randy has written nearly fifty books, including *Heaven*, *The Treasure Principle*, and the award-winning novel *Safely Home*. His books have sold more than nine million copies and have been translated into more than sixty languages.

Randy has written for many magazines, including EPM's *Eternal Perspectives*. He blogs, is active on Facebook and Twitter, and has been a guest on more than seven hundred radio, television, and online programs.

Randy resides in Gresham, Oregon, with his wife, Nanci. They have two married daughters and are the proud grandparents of five grandsons. Randy enjoys spending time with his family, biking, underwater photography, research, and reading.

You may contact Eternal Perspective Ministries at www.epm.org or 39085 Pioneer Blvd., Suite 206, Sandy, OR 97055 or 503-668-5200. Follow Randy on Facebook: www.facebook.com/randyalcorn, on Twitter: www.twitter.com/randyalcorn, and on his blog: www.epm.org/blog.